NO QUIET END

Brian Dennis Hartford

Original Poems by: Brian Dennis Hartford © 2024
Original Cover Art by: Brian Dennis Hartford © 2024
H. publications is Registered Self-Publishing Trademark of Brain Dennis Hartford

All rights reserved. No part of this book may be reproduced in any form or by any means without the prior written consent of the author, with the sole exception for brief quotes used in reviews of book. The right to litigation will be fully exercised in any or all cases involving intellectual or graphic design property theft or unauthorized of author's original content.

Warning: These poems may contain adult content, sexually graphic material, and some violence.

ISBN-13: 979-8-9857314-5-3

First Printing: March 2024

10 9 8 7 6 5 4 3 2 1

Printed in the United States of America

INTRODUCTION

"There cannot be a quiet end..." I had heard once, from someone, somewhere. Maybe it was an uncle, or my father's best friend, whom I still fondly remember, Sam. Perhaps it was one of his friends, Chris, or Tink, or Bill, or God knows the multitudes of characters that I had kept company at such a young age. Or, perhaps it was a junkie on the streets of Albuquerque, or a drunk at some random bar, or just me trying to convince myself, there were still more grander things to come. I remember not, but here I am at fifty-five, and I wonder, will there be a quiet end? Or a grand end? Might I pass in such a way that the world will know of it. Even if it might be just one great written line. What will it be, I wonder that will inspire? Or am I doomed to a quiet death as all the rest. Words and a life to be buried and long forgotten, save for some old book on a shelf no one read.

And so, here I am, yet another poem book. I've moved to Europe. Sold everything to follow a dream that seems dimmer to achieve now, than whence before I left to chase after it. A life far from quiet in the moment that is for sure. So, forgive the turmoil of the rhyme, of the sequence in which each poem is set, but it is in there that the narrative of my life at that moment lay. The narrative of remembering, of love, and lust, and reckless romances. Of sad reckoning and of long soulful goodbyes.

Enjoy!

To Sam, and all the rest.

CONTENTS

THERE CANNOT BE A QUIET END	1
WRITING IS A NOONTIME AFFAIR	3
BETTER THEM THAN YOU	5
ONE LAST DRINK OF "PROMISE"	7
WHERE THE RED TAIL HAWKS FLY	9
WHEN A HOUSE BECOMES A HOME	11
I FOUND THE DEVIL ON THE STREETS OF ZWEIBRÜCKEN TONIGHT	13
WHERE THE CROWS NEST	15
FALL IN BERLIN	17
WE ARE BUT ACTORS, IN THE GREAT SNUFF FILM CALLED LIFE	19
FROM PARIS TO PAIA	21
THE OLD FILIPINO MAN ON THE ROADSIDE BY WOOLWORTH'S KAIMUKI	25
IT'S ALWAYS THE OTHER... (THAT THE OTHER HAD WANTED)	27
LEONNI	29
VERONICA	31
15 MINUTES	33
JUST WAITING FOR A FIRST HELLO (AGAIN)	35
WITH HEARTS LIKE OURS	37
A TONGUE SET LOOSE UPON FORBIDDEN PLACES	39
CAREFULL OF THE BONES	41
VIOLET WAS THE COLOR OF MY DEATH	43
JUST WAITING FOR THIS ROCK TO SLIDE INTO THE SEA	45
IN WATERS DEEP AND SINFUL	47
MAYBE ITS THESE WORDS THAT WILL MAKE ME FAMOUS	49

WHAT GOOD ARE WINGS	51
"SOMETIME…"	53
JUST A FLAME IS AS ANY OTHER LIGHTER	55
ELYXIR	57
IN THE COLOR WHERE DEATH GETS LOST	59
"AI ŢIGARĂ?"	61
AND SO, I WILL PLACE FLOWERS UPON MY OWN GRAVE	63
AT THIS CAFE THE OTHER DAY	65
IF FALL HAD WAITED ONE MORE DAY	67
RUBUS	69
TO WHERE THE CLOUDS GO, THAT I WILL NEVER SEE	71
THAT DAY IN MADRID	73
PERFECT IS AN AGONIZINGLY INDESCRIBABLE THING	75
IN THE EVENT OF A NUCLEAR ATTACK	77
THE SONG I ALMOST LEFT YOU BY	79
MY IMMORTAL TORNIQUET	81
ANNA CURVĂ	83
WAYANG ANGEL	85
JUST ONE MINUTE LONGER	87
LOST TO YOU	89
SOMETIMES, LOVE HAS AN END	91
A MILLION MORE PENNIES	93
"Proshchay, moya dorogaya…"	95
REPLACED	97
IMMORTAL, I TREAD	99
A PECULIAR SHADE OF RED	101

THERE CANNOT BE A QUIET END

Cigars

What is it about them?

Conjuring up the image of dirty old men and Thailand whores

Bar-side in some forgotten place

An uncle comes to mind

Sam.

That nostalgia as a young lad

Though he smoked Marlboros

And drank cheap gin exclusively

Still...

It's there, in the wisping smoke of my cigar

Poems, yeah, he read them

Gave them new meaning

Gave them the ugly truth of it

Words were cruel in his recital

But it gave hope enough

I miss those days

Shipyards and construction sites

And seedy bars where maybe a ten-year-old should not be

But there I was

Smoking bubble gum cigarettes and drinking Shirley Temples

A man had standards you know
I don't think they had bubblegum cigars
Or, maybe, I wasn't deemed ready for that yet
And I was surrounded by beautiful women
Hard drinking, smoking, cussing women
My mother was their queen
The delicate flower that was deathly poison to taste
A slight smile smoking and indifferent to any and all
And the men smoked and drank, plotting new adventures and quick money schemes which slowly turned to a quiet life at home
To retirements
And in the end, little deaths
And now men don't even dream
Nor the women they keep
None really knows the meaning of "king" or "queen"
So, if you ever wanted to know just a little bit more of me
There it is;
Bubblegum cigarettes and Sherly Temples turned cigars and rum and poetry
And an ever-running away from such quiet ends as they.

WRITING IS A NOONTIME AFFAIR

It's noon

And a fifth glass of wine goes down faster than the first, in the garden of Eden

Eve lays naked and golden poolside

My eyes trace the curves of her body

If she could turn to marble, she'd sell for a billion dollars

Michelangelo might make the claim it was his work

Another glass

A Cuban cigar to contemplate the grass growing undaunted by the coming of winter

The roses struggle to remain regal

While the acorns fall intently aimless

Leaves

It's God's way of saying you won't make it long

Eve turns over

Life is a bore

Another glass

And one more paragraph

Perhaps in a few hours

I'll write some more

Maybe Eve can decide the fate of fiction

Maybe not

But we'll try just the same

Eve lights a cigarette;

"Je m'ennuie, qu'allons-nous faire ce soir?"

Sometimes, Eden is hell, just by a prettier name.

ONE LAST DRINK OF "PROMISE"

It's something that shouldn't have been said
But that's the way of us
Lips upon our broken champagne glasses, cheering the other on anyways
While beneath; we're seething
Bleeding
A half blood, half champagne cocktail
We'll call it *"Promise"*
The bittersweet truth of us
Somewhere, the lie is lost
Yet so close
Drop by drop upon the white crisp linen napkin
That is our make believe;
Us
This you and I
Parched lips upon a jagged champagne glass
Hearts near drained, but still wanting in bleeding
Ever lost in the thirsting
Of us and one last drink for the road.

WHERE THE RED TAIL HAWKS FLY

Just sitting here watching a last sunset

On an old horse

On an old trail

That ends up in old towns

With old Spanish names

The Indians made them

The Conquistadors Sainted them

The hunger for gold and silver forged them

Forges them still

Like spurs driving into dying flesh

A six-gun fires

The kid's drunk again

Angry

We're all angry here

Desperate

Beneath a watermelon mountain

Before the sea of the west, winding thinner with the years

But still,

We've laid down lifetimes here

All buried on a hill somewhere

Nameless

Soon to be as the sun

Marching hopeful into another; *"One last time"*

Over dry grassy hills and juniper shrubs

Where our shadow stains like blood

Yep,

That's what I believe I said the last time

"One last time"

The draw;

Blinded

For I could never quite get over how beautifully indifferent the Red Tail hawks are flying effortlessly, above, in the turquoise sky.

What was it that was written on our gravestones again?

Oh, yeah; "Pals"

I had almost forgot.

WHEN A HOUSE BECOMES A HOME

The key turns

And in the throw of a bolt

My heart died a little more

Piece by piece she's packed away

Boxed and breathless

Waiting

The unavoidable parting

The blinds are drawn

Blinded to the flowers in the garden

And the stars at night that show

To the laughter in the love shack

To shadows playing in the water

To the dreamer that had forged her soul

A few months will turn to years

I know

Her heart still boxed and breathless

Waiting

Wanting of a grand return

Such is the sacrifice of a house I've come to love and to know as simply *home*.

I FOUND THE DEVIL ON THE STREETS OF ZWEIBRÜCKEN TONIGHT

I found the devil on the streets tonight
Down, where two rivers collide
On a bridge, hesitant to give way to yesteryear
In the light of a faltering streetlamp
I knew in her smile that we had meet before
Same place
Another time and night
When the Romans had built this place
And Napoleon camped here once
Where the Zia had rose but never set
Casting shadowed hands upon the wire
Such is history and all its claims of grandeur
And we kissed in the shadows, hypocrites
What was that moment when
Amidst the bombs falling
You said; "See you then!"
And seated at the end of a bar
There you are!
In a blue leather jacket
Just as you were then

Just as you are now

For at the end of all things then,

And I know, now

Was the Devil of Zweibrücken.

WHERE THE CROWS NEST

We are a walk along the river where the crow's nest
Exposed upon barren trees, for spring cannot seem to free itself of winter
And the river below flows dirty
Sort of hopeless
I think
A surrender to another's ambition, perhaps
But I stop and watch just the same
Lean upon the wrought iron rail of yesteryear
Strain to see if rainbow trout or spotted browns still reside in the depths below
But the water runs grey and brown, long dead
A drifting mirror
Where my own reflection looks back to me, pondering of the apparition above
The eyes there
Set against a scarf and high felt Petty Coat collar, contemplating
And she comes to stand beside me
Silent and expecting

In a cheap long coat ringed in faux fur with hands plunged in deep pockets to ward against the lifeless cold

"Was siehst du?" She spoke, expecting some inciteful answer

"Just a slow dying..." I turned with a forced smile

"Ein Date für die Nacht? Zweihundert Euro!"

"Sure, I've got some time. As much, if not more, than the river has." I replied

Beneath, where the crows upon leafless trees had long found their sleepless rest.

FALL IN BERLIN

The leaves lay gentle upon the cobblestone

Yellow, gold, and red

Indifferent to the ashes of a city in ruin

To the bodies heaped in unmarked graves

To the bombers overhead

To any victor

To any defeated

To any who did not listen to the poets.

And here we are, again

Fall in Berlin

Indifferent leaves

Falling hapless

Expectant that the winds will take them away from here

But it doesn't

Instead,

Just the old familiar bed of cobblestone

Cold and damp

Set above the bones of yesteryear

Where the leaves fall indifferent as they always have and always will

Berlin.

WE ARE BUT ACTORS, IN THE GREAT SNUFF FILM CALLED LIFE

We found each other in a place that would make the Devil blush

There was no sex

Only, the lingering smoke of cigarettes and Absinth

No words were spoken

Because we already knew

Just a long pause to watch the world

Its ugly truth, high above the ramparts across from where God had failed

That was our measure

She and I

For one does not fuck in the coming of the end

But rather, that is the intercourse

Remaining idle at the end of all things as the hand of fate, itself dying, constricts about your neck

The pleasure is in the letting go

That is the cum

Life is little more than an elaborate snuff film, we had both agreed

And our fine crystal glasses clinked, in a silent cheer again

Our eyes set back to watch the sun go down

Our death play's final curtain call.

FROM PARIS TO PAIA

Sugar, it's why they came

A last chance at paradise

With white shirts turned red from the dirt and sweat

Blood and a thousand cuts

There's never time to sharpen blades

It only gets harder

Hemo! they slave

And up over the hill, the fire comes

An inferno

Burning, absolute burning

Hell, is the best description

The crackling of it, insidious

Like in the end, where redemption finally catches up with the flesh

On Saturday night, they gather

Old Paia Town theatre

A buck gets a drink and pork noodles

Or Manapua, or Tripe Stew on rice

A ticket is twenty-five cents!

And soon she'll sing for them

The China doll princess of Paia

Cloaked in a bleach white dress

Long white satin gloves

Black ankle long hair coiled up high upon her head

Held fast with pearl inlaid chopsticks

A faint smile as she positions upon gaslight lit stage

An avalanche she looks

Grand and animated

She had been a concubine in Paris, you know

Some French lord they say

The group falls silent before her unearthly beauty

Her emeralds and diamonds blaze

The goddess Pele has nothing on the image

Hearts pound

The cigarette smoke and humidity give way to hope again

To a dream life

Where she is their wife

And they live on manager row

The lights dim

A chord is struck

"Parlez-moi d'amour!"

Her mouth forms the first words

Sweet and elegant, and some say

Unearthly

The silence falls, deafening

The anticipation agonizing

She could be my wife, you know!"

They'll later brag

But she won't

Never be

A body soon to be sunk by a jealous husband into the sea

And her hands, small and delicate place upon the microphone

A new song now

The ugly truth of a life set to word upon red lips and an angelic voice

"Nous ne sommes que des fantômes parmi la canne..."

She laments to a lone off-key guitar

"We are all but ghost amongst the cane..."

Hemo!

And white shirts turn a darker red

The blades still need sharpening

But there's no time now

The fire is coming!

THE OLD FILIPINO MAN ON THE ROADSIDE BY WOOLWORTH'S KAIMUKI

There's just this old chair now
And the sugar cane has long since gone wild
Pineapples were another thing entirely
"Eh! Boy, you get dolla'? Like buy mangos?"

IT'S ALWAYS THE OTHER...(THAT THE OTHER HAD WANTED)

Alone in the shitter

Below, where toilet paper and a turd still lingers

His hands, callus on my neck

My hands determined on his

And in the right twist upon the voice box, brings about breathlessness

His teeth upon my stomach

His teeth upon my zipper

Outside she waits

Engaged in her own debate

Hair tangles faces

Belt buckles struggle

Both in their own battle

Who is against the wall

Who prevails

Each, the other, wanting of what lay just beyond the wall

Each, the other, wanting of those teeth upon their stomach

Each the slave of fate

Each the slave of want

Each left to the thoughts of the other's, other

And upon the wall

He descends

She descends

Eyes closed in imagination of another

Such is the play;

The other always gets what the other had wanted.

LEONNI

"Would someone write about me?
Let them know that I am a woman
Have a voice
Have this thing
Romance, is it this hard?
A long walk in the park
Just hold my hand
I don't want to fuck
I have the same dreams as you
A nightmare for me, really
Playing out in my head
Of this one moment, when
The world might listen once
Because I said "I do!"
I'm only twenty
But I feel a hundred
I just want a choice
To be held with no conditions
To not be judged
This thing inside
And I tried

But found my hand left empty
My walk in the park a cemetery
Where dreams can't help but die
In the want of many
Would you write about me
Anyone?"

───────────────

And so, I write of you tonight, Leonni
These words
The words you spoke
And in so doing, relinquish you
Not in the name of any love
But in the name of you
Your voice
That you have these dreams
And that I stand not the gate
But the sentinel by which you pass
Protected and unhindered
For that is the sacrifice
Lust or love for voice
And so, make it the grandest voice
So that the world knows I did not pass in vain.

VERONICA

They asked me for a poem
Of some memory long ago
And the image came of you
Of a night when;
A cigarette hung from your lips
Hair blond in parts and uncommitted mascara dripped
The thick red of your lipstick smeared
How many did you blow?
How many did you fuck?
What was their promise, after?
But your hand-drawn heart proposition
Betrayed the real need
And, they asked me to write a poem
Of a moment between you and I
Loners in the flooding world
Of a moment that could have been
But held our truth in the passing of a cigarette
The only kiss we knew that mattered then
And they asked me to write a poem
Of something that had happened once
And there you were all of a sudden

The infamous Veronica

In your hand-drawn heart proposition

And a chance we knew we both might miss

A momentary love we shall always have in the smoke blown from your cigarette

Because blow jobs are for the uninitiated

Not a love as this.

15 MINUTES

You've got fifteen minutes to bleed the truth

A minute's view in which to tell the world your heart is dying

Two at best, if you're a lucky one

Before they scroll on

And it's gone

The voice you had

Lost into the rest

Clamoring

This is the truth of us

The truth of you

The truth of me

This one eternal hopeful moment

Dependent on curiosity

And then we're gone

Forever

Forgotten

Deleted...

This is the truth of us.

JUST WAITING FOR A FIRST HELLO (AGAIN)

Don't mind me

I'm just waiting for our first *"Hello"*

It's been a while

But I can wait some more

Will it be at some Cafe in Paris

On the ramparts of Bran

Amidst the Heather upon the moor

Egypt again might be more befitting

Babylon don't exist anymore

I love it when you walk by close

That reassuring devilish smile

That the end of time will be well worth the wait

A first time in your arms, again

As the curtain falls

The sun has four point five billion years yet to go

What will that first kiss be like, you think

Yeah, times on our side

That last second will be our forever

A constellation in the stars

For them to marvel by

For them to find love by

For them...yeah, we've got to wait...for them to find the other by.

WITH HEARTS LIKE OURS

How hard do we make this?
Just push me against the wall
Pin my wrists
Outside the bar door
Just out of view
Your "friends" won't know
Under the lone streetlight
Where the broken bottle glass grinds
And a taxicab on the corner waits
Fuck the games
I know you like girls
But we've got this thing don't we
Anger
Hatred
A wish to see the world end in flames
Well, girl, we are the flame
A single moment against a brick wall
Ignite it, or not
It's the best we've got
It's the best we'll do tonight
There ain't nobody else with hearts like ours

Rabid

Insatiable

Destruction

Are you out?

Or, are you in, TONIGHT!

A TONGUE SET LOOSE UPON FORBIDDEN PLACES

And I'm here now

A reflection in the mirror of your boudoir

To trace the outline of a shadow

To trace the outline of a promise

And I'm here now

A tongue long bound for forbidden places

So, the vial, will tell the world

And I'm gone now

Dead in the desire of a forbidden place.

CAREFULL OF THE BONES

Two cigarettes were left to smolder

And an unfinished glass of wine waited patiently

As their reflections stretched out upon it in passing

The scene; two lovers leaving a bar

Was any need see

Though they never care to look

Never bother to know anymore

"Careful of the bones…"

He spoke calmly

"I always am…"

She smiled back thoughtful, kissing him

"For the bones are the story of your life, my love."

VIOLET WAS THE COLOR OF MY DEATH

And I write of this

From a place beyond the window, where the lighting finds its way hurried and threatening across the late-night sky

The rain, dreary and deadfall taps relentless against my

window

Like that angry incessant raven in that Poe poem

An echo of a night ages ago

Your heels upon the cobblestone

As my tongue emerges slightly, to soothe this ages old wound upon my lips

A memento of a kiss I should have passed upon

But chose not

And now in the shadow with pen in hand I still stumble to make reason of the alleyway called life

For poetry long gave way to Absinth and Cointreau driven dementia, and laudanum filled veins

The only words left, as worn out as the fist

Thrown up in the vomit

A rejection of a hollowed stomach bent upon the beating

And a dead heart dry and motionless

And I write

Write of this one moment

When all my words had come true of you

When upon this street somewhere in a place I cannot now remember

In a place now so long lost

Where the sounds of night had once been comforting

Became a terror

At the time when the world begins its awakening to start again its long day dying

There, unexpected, you were

And the lightning flashes across the window becoming temporally, the color of your eyes that night

The color of truth of which now the ink writes

My death and the color for which I shall forever know it by;

Violet.

JUST WAITING FOR THIS ROCK TO SLIDE INTO THE SEA

I sat dreaming for when this rock might fall into the sea

Watched the fissure grow millimeter by millimeter

Day by day, hour by hour

Agonizing really

The shedding of weight

The unburdening of life

Was this rock a cancer, I wondered of the cliff above

To the mountain

Or, was it a failed dream

A surrender

A slow suicide

The desire to become something smaller and less magnificent

Because standing tall is a death in its own right.

And I sit, patiently awaiting the day when the decision is finally made

And a rock simply slides into the sea.

IN WATERS DEEP AND SINFUL

Tonight, we tasted waters deep and sinful

Beneath the judgement curtain

Upon the alter-bed

Drank of the Devil's wine

Though, I might argue that it of was God's making

But our tongues cared not

Tracing our desires upon her skin

Long and lingering

A cryptic message in the moment, of lust

Meant for none other but for the reader

Soon evaporated as does the rain on the heated dune

And in her;

We had drowned all too willingly.

MAYBE ITS THESE WORDS THAT WILL MAKE ME FAMOUS

There was no words

Just a broken heart

Walking below the streetlights

Amidst the shadows of wanting

A reflection of anyone

In the Diner window

An empty cup of coffee gone uncollected upon the counter

And the apron hangs

Hangs upon the hook

It's 5 AM anywhere

And a heart is broken

Wishing to die.

WHAT GOOD ARE WINGS

What good are wings
When you're in a pool
Flap them all you want
You're not getting out
No, just suspended in flight
Flapping aimless
Dead, but you don't know it yet
Flying, but not getting anywhere
Life
The abyss below
The abyss above
But going nowhere
A shoreline on all sides
But just too distant to make
So, I fly frantic
Terrified of the abyss
Trying not to sink
But unable to catch air
This is life now
Just a fly or something, flapping frantic in a pool somewhere
Unable to escape.

"SOMETIME…"

Let's have lunch sometime

Not now, nor not never

But sometime

A bistro in France, I think

A back alley one

In a lost town

A town no one goes to anymore

Perhaps, even, from since the war

Maybe there's a tiny garden

With lavender and roses

Maybe not

The chairs will wobble

The table, crooked

An unknown wine

Mismatched glasses

And you'll sit across from me

A smirk slowly turning to smile

As the tips of your high-heels point accusingly

Yeah, that's me

As I've always been

No lies

Just this dreamer lost to your smile

To the storm in your eyes

And a chance at "sometime…"

JUST A FLAME IS AS ANY OTHER LIGHTER

I watched the ash of her cigarette fall as she flicked it off the end, as if dead snow upon the cobblestone

Her face framed indifferent in black and sable mink, as her hand placed my lighter in her coat pocket

"A flame is as if any other, dear…"

She exhaled, turning to leave

It's got to die out sometime."

ELYXIR

If I could write the scene of our bodies

What would the calligraphy say

Better yet, a painting

Set in the deepest shadow

Four bodies finding bliss upon the bed of proposition

The brush, my tongue

Slowly making its way across the canvas

The only colors need be captured

That of heated flesh

Reflected in beads of sweat

Swathed upon sheets of red

Waves set to storm upon a shore at last sunset

Or could it be the camera

Stop action snapshots

Through the keyhole

From beyond the glass

Where the black light knows best the frame

Desperate in the capture of the image

Anticipative of the end

But the film roll runs out

Yet the play remains

Actors oblivious to the spectators

An impromptu script re-write

Raw upon the stage

Live for all to see

Lost souls caught in the final moments

Found in the Elyxir of ecstasy

And if you could know the scene of our bodies

Would you join in our play?

IN THE COLOR WHERE DEATH GETS LOST

The lightening plays across the night sky chasing after nothing out, beyond, over a cottage covered hillside

While down in the blue room

The wind blows wild through the curtain-veil

Dancing ghosts, fleeing before her

But bound to witness by the hook and rod

Held fast to the horror

And upon the black bed

The color of death gets lost

Drop by drop

A heart anesthetized, immobile

A mouth open, but unable

In breath nor sound

And outside the lightening played across the night sky chasing after nothing

Beyond a cottage covered hillside

Where a knock on a door had invited in love for a moment.

"AI ȚIGARĂ?"

A white hand finds its way down the stairway banister

Black nails gliding just above the wrought Nouveau steel

Where the full moon beams down through a window high above

Highlighting black heeled boots tip-toeing silent upon the fine marble step

And above they lay as if fast asleep

Two pallid statues embraced idol and veiled beneath red silk sheets

Lost to the depths of her lure beneath a street lamp

And the question;

"Bună ziua, aveți o țigară?"

AND SO, I WILL PLACE FLOWERS UPON MY OWN GRAVE

My hands push upon the lid

A statue frozen in decay

Forced to watch the ages

A hundred different lifetimes

Another chance to make the case

Another chance to miss parole

Just this sound of God's gavel set upon a headstone framed

Framed against a sunrise

Its echo that of footsteps upon a million dead roses

Each petal a petition

Scribed by the living

And signed by the shovel.

And so, I will place flowers upon my own grave

Thank you very much.

AT THIS CAFE THE OTHER DAY

"Ein Pilsner, danke. Und ein Wasser ohne Gas, zwei Gläser."

So, the standard goes for me

Lost and writing of life in this German town

While waiting on this girl I met, drunk in a bar

The Hobbit, I think

Or, was it Drumm

Sutter, maybe

I don't know

It's Sumner

It's hot

It's Humid

The storm clouds were gathering again

Sweat darkens my shirt

Will she show?

My mind ponders

It's been quite a few years

Give or take

I don't know

Time means little here

A young man off in war

A young girl in the ruin

And then, here we are

Wanting of a lunch, maybe more

The church bells chime in High Noon

Noon

Was it noon?

"Hallo, hey, ich bin hier…" she says clad in this flowery dress, cheerful and smiling

The ensuing silence deafening

As deafening as the day, the bullets came

As deafening as her screams standing over me

As deafening as the war raged, and the bombs fell all around us

"Was sollen wir essen?"

And it was the most beautiful lunch

With a view of the place that I had died once

Only, she didn't know this

Or, did she?

We ghosts are a most complicated thing.

IF FALL HAD WAITED ONE MORE DAY

I had found this leaf in a stream

Not floating hopeful

But drown

Drug down upon the bottom, across and over the river stone

Helpless to the current

Where the cold waits, patient

For if only Fall could have waited one more day

Who knows, maybe this story might have been different.

RUBUS

I sit, high up in a window,

Watching the garden grow wild from neglect,

Day by day, inch by inch,

Each plant choked out from the other, crowding,

And there from within the green depths,

Just below the reds and purples, and yellows and whites and hope and joy and bumbling bees and butterfly's,

Lurks the Rubus slithering with the intent that it shall be the beautiful one.

Its thorny grasp, working its way from above and below and in between

And from every side,

From miles and miles, it has come to smother out its detractors.

And there, around a little pond

Some flowers can still reach out over, hopeful,

Temporarily escaping the inevitable,

Little petal-tears fallen, floating upon the water-lily sky, where the Koi lumber on oblivious to sinking tides,

While dragonfly's, dew laden, wait for the morning fog to lift its veil from over the sun.

None can escape this, I think,

I know,

Not even the Rubus.

And so, I choose to take a nap instead,

For the garden can wait another day, I hope.

TO WHERE THE CLOUDS GO, THAT I WILL NEVER SEE

The clouds march purposeful across blue sky

"To where might they be going?"

Was the only thought

Of a boy dying in the mud upon the barbed wire

Amidst the whistle calls to victory

Now, but a discarded marionet

"To be as them..."

Was his last thought

My last thought

I know all too well now.

THAT DAY IN MADRID

A war was coming

Change was coming

All seemed this Cano color palate just on the verge of turning to black and white photographs and a headline

And there she was

Leading the strike

Sweat yellowed blouse

Men's twill trousers tied fast with this big leather belt, its tail wrapped back halfway around, and pant legs rolled up not once, not twice, but at least five times, over big black work boots worn to the shank

And she brandished an iron pipe

And a sign that simply read; "¡CAMBIO!"

And there I was, high on the sixth floor

In a window typing this very poem

When the gun shots rang out

And so, on that day in Madrid

I never loved any other again.

PERFECT IS AN AGONIZINGLY INDESCRIBABLE THING

And the days pass,

Just waiting for the words to describe the way you felt beneath my fingertips, as I caressed your skin again after so many years.

That feeling, still as if it were yesterday,

When we were delicate and purposeful

Though we knew there was an end.

And a million more hours pass

Tracing the feel of you in the dark

Over, again and again

What words describe?

Electrifying maybe

Comfort without doubt

That we had been here always, most defiantly

And still here

Caught again in a temporary moment before your body pulls away from me

My fingers left suspended

And the words aren't there

For perfect truly is an agonizingly indescribable thing.

IN THE EVENT OF A NUCLEAR ATTACK

Fuck it!

It's just us now

So, let's make us famous

A tribute to the final minutes

Set to stone for a thousand years

To be found under the rubble of yesteryear

Dried and petrified

Intertwined

Naked

Fearless in our fate

Embraced upon a bed

Champagne bottles all around

The good stuff, because there would be no bill to pay

Caught in the act

Caught in what might have saved the day

If they only could have found a way

Might be France this time

Might be Spain

Might be Tahiti, or some other place

Just this sculpture now

Made of bone and ash

A soon to be a number one tourist destination
And they will speculate
And they will converse
And write papers about the last moment of our lives
The most romantic stories
Of how we had chosen not to run nor hide
But defy the fire
Amid the ruin of ambition
So, yeah, let's set that date!
Let's do this for them
One last pose, for future-kind
Three hearts beating fearless in the death of the world
Drunk and laughing
A love cast immortal at the edge of annihilation
We, the new Pompeiians.

THE SONG I ALMOST LEFT YOU BY

There was this song I almost left you by

The sound of the needle on the B side still scratching in my mind

Suitcase on the sidewalk

An impatient Taxi driver

A frozen shadow in the doorway

"Just give us the night, I'll make I right..."

Beyond, the streetlights had seemed such a promise

"Just give us the night, I'll make it right..."

A freedom I hadn't known for a while

"Just give us some time, I'll make it right..."

A chance to stand on my own a while

"Just give us the night..."

And a Taxi Cab's taillights soon fade away empty down city streets

And a defeated suitcase sits idle in the rain

"I'm gonna' make it all right..."

And bed sheets fall upon our bodies

"Just give us a bit more time..."

And two hearts try to find their rhythm again

"Just a bit more...time."

She smiles, kissing my fears away

"Just a bit more…time…"

And freedom was let slip to sleep.

"Just give us the night, it will be alright…"

MY IMMORTAL TORNIQUET

And your lips had found their place

Perfectly.

ANNA CURVĂ

Think I'm ready for the death kiss

The last kiss

The forever kiss

The kiss that crushes kiss

Slow

And deep

And lingering

A talented tongue

An intent tongue

The tongue that will make me forget, everything

The tongue that throws down the final challenge

Cross over now or, be left behind forever

For the threshold of crossing and staying are pretty close, if not the same

I'd say

So, make it sweet my love

Make it last

Let me look into those sad eyes

As I trace the longing upon your face

As I touch that part of your lip, behind where lay a missing fang

Let me feel your breath gentle upon my cheek

Cognac and cigarettes

There under the red light

Upon your bed

A black sea

You, the taker of the lost into the underworld

And I will go willingly despite an early age

The only price

The ticket for entry

The full surrender of my soul

The keeper's price

Such a small price, really

For an eternity in you

Anna Curvă.

WAYANG ANGEL

The whip falls upon the skin
A body straining amid the candlelight
A shadow, stretched out upon the wall
A puppet bound in silk ropes upon the hook
Where its feet are held just above the fire
Precarious in the image of prayer
Wanting of the atonement
Wanting of the revelation
And the whip falls, again
The sound of penance
Of desire
Of freedom
Of a love not found anywhere else
For the flesh feels more than the spirit, I know
And the whip falls again
And again
And again
And again
And again…

JUST ONE MINUTE LONGER

Give us just one minute longer

Take another breath

Let our fingers linger upon the others

Held up to the light

Maybe we are the ones

I think the clock knows

A shy smile

And this sadness in your eyes

We don't have to talk

Just breathe

In this room, we are safe one minute longer than all the rest

So, stay

For me

For you

For us

Just one minute longer

I promise, I know

That in that last fleeting second

We will find forever.

LOST TO YOU

I'm not the best romantic

Can't get right a single line

Just a million paper napkins, with a word or two

Fallen upon an old bar floor

Some effort to describe this love we had

Now ringed in a whisky glass brand

Maybe the words will come right someday

Perhaps everything I've written, all got lost in you

Carried out the front door one by one

Stuck to the souls of patron's shoes

Left curbside

White leaves blowing

Silent in the sound of your cab driving away

To fall dead again upon empty city streets

Taking their rightful place amid the fall leaves turned orange and red

Where all my best words lay with you

Wet and clinging in the winter rains, washing steady towards the drain

Maybe they'll make it to the sea someday

Maybe not…

"Möchten Sie einen weiteren?"

"Ja, warum nicht?"

"Bonjour, cette place est-elle occupée?" She cut in,

"Nein, no, please, take a seat, I'm ready for the next line..."

SOMETIMES, LOVE HAS AN END

Sometimes, love has an end

Love runs out

Runs its course

Like the mountain snows that become a raging river

But just a trickle by the time it gets to the sea

Just this wetland place

Where, the waves don't take any notice

And one's ankles won't even get wet

Yet, there, a picture-perfect picnic will be set

An umbrella and basket

Champagne and a ring

Amid a sunny day and the sea grasses swaying in a hopeful salt scented breeze

And a sunhat is clutched in anticipation as tears of joy fall

And the promise of forever still lies; *"I do!"*

And becomes a mighty river again

Flowing fast and fervid

At least until the flatlands

Maybe until the desert

Maybe through the concrete canals

But always ending just out of reach of the sea

A sort of petering death

Like watercolor spreading out upon a white page

Until the ink meets its match within the fiber

Clawing for a moment then just stops

Gives up

Yeah, sometimes, love has an end

But its ok

You and me

We'll find another river.

A MILLION MORE PENNIES

A penny descends

Hapless to the river currents below

A mere glint, fast fading

Swallowed up in the turbulence

Drug down and across the bottom

Pulled fast from the streetlight-stars above

But soon to be found again, someday

In a wish that was once made

Soon to be found again, someday

In two strangers upon a bridge

Who somehow now, from out of a million pennies, found a first kiss

Where green eyes and a hopeful smile was held framed in gentle hands

Making wishes again...

And I'd cast a million more pennies for this one moment with you, again

And then a million more.

"Proshchay, moya dorogaya..."

Outside an early morning rain finds its way upon the fog shrouded cobblestone

The city silent in its grey

I watch as she turns up the collar of her coat

Sometimes, the only goodbye is in the sound a hotel door quietly closing makes.

REPLACED

The image was little more than a facade
Love didn't have a chance
Lust even less fortunate
Me just walking with my head down in the rain
Maybe my tears will find "the one"
Somewhere in a rain puddle
A raindrop perhaps
Or another as itself
Just left lost dancing alone in the depths of a temporary sea
The discarded of the storm
The discarded of the heart
It's anybody's guess anymore
But the drain looms ever near, there's no denying
Maybe there's still a chance
Maybe not
The sea is a long way off
And indifference has long killed any hope.

IMMORTAL, I TREAD

And beneath the lid of time,
What was,
Was little more than what might have been.
And what might have been,
Never really was.
So, invite such peaceful sleep,
For when it comes time for what might be, again,
Lay only another shade of hell to tread.

A PECULIAR SHADE OF RED

Go on, cast your wishes

See where the rain takes them

Down, along ancient marble streets

Where above, ornate spired-dreams slowly erode

Drop by drop

Grain by grain

Hope; the grand limestone fantasy

For age kills dreams

Kills reason

Kills any further passion

Eventually

And I pass in my black suit

Unnoticed, mostly

Despite my tie, this peculiar shade of red

A sea of flesh parting

All but ghosts, really

Trapped to this city-place

To any place

And there she sits

My wayward angel

With black wings folded

At the end of a bar long closed

With an old familiar grin

As she sips at her rouge Absinth and gin

The only reflections that matter

She and I, through the wall of glass where raindrops find their death

Slipping one by one into the drains bellow

Quiet and hopeless

A faint gurgling

The sound of forever closing

And we won't meet

Nor share a drink

Nor speak of anything

Just two silent knowing faces

A cigar salute and a raised glass

To us, the window shadows waiting for our ends

Quiet or otherwise

Save for our peculiar shade of red.

The Author

Brian Dennis Hartford is a published author and writer of fiction, romance, and poetry. He has a bachelor's degree in security management and has worked in the private security industry for over twenty years. He currently resides in Europe.

A Special Thanks

To my wife, family, and friends who have made this all possible. To Anna, past, present and future, even if for but a fleeting moment. To Sam and all the rest. To Hlieb, waiting on some words my friend. To Gasthaus Hobbit, keeper of we the hopeless souls. And lastly, to Veronica, and this one moment long ago.

Cover Photo Source Credits

Photo by Brian Dennis Hartford. Lee'Ann at The Hobbit, Zweibrücken, sometime around 2 AM, 2023.

www.ingramcontent.com/pod-product-compliance
Lightning Source LLC
Chambersburg PA
CBHW032129090426
42743CB00007B/525